AF228528

FC CINCINNATI

BY CHRIS ADAMSKI

SportsZone

An Imprint of Abdo Publishing
abdobooks.com

abdobooks.com

Published by Abdo Publishing, a division of ABDO, PO Box 398166, Minneapolis, Minnesota 55439. Copyright © 2022 by Abdo Consulting Group, Inc. International copyrights reserved in all countries. No part of this book may be reproduced in any form without written permission from the publisher. SportsZone™ is a trademark and logo of Abdo Publishing.

Printed in the United States of America, North Mankato, Minnesota
052021
092021

Cover Photo: Rich Graessle/Icon Sportswire/AP Images
Interior Photos: Ian Johnson/Icon Sportswire/AP Images, 5, 6, 19, 23, 39; John Minchillo/ AP Images, 9, 10–11, 14–15, 27, 30, 33, 34, 36–37; Kevin Schultz/Cal Sport Media/Zuma Wire/AP Images, 13, 24; Kirk Irwin/Getty Images Sport/Getty Images, 16; Richard Drew/ AP Images, 20; Rich von Biberstein/Icon Sportswire/AP Images, 29; Jason Whitman/Getty Images Sport/Getty Images, 40; Pro Shots/Sipa USA/AP Images, 43

Editor: Patrick Donnelly
Series Designer: Dan Peluso

Library of Congress Control Number: 2020948261

Publisher's Cataloging-in-Publication Data

Names: Adamski, Chris, author.
Title: FC Cincinnati / by Chris Adamski
Description: Minneapolis, Minnesota : Abdo Publishing, 2022 | Series: Inside MLS |
    Includes online resources and index.
Identifiers: ISBN 9781532194726 (lib. bdg.) | ISBN 9781098214388 (ebook)
Subjects: LCSH: Soccer teams--Juvenile literature. | Professional sports franchises--
    Juvenile literature. | Sports Teams--Juvenile literature.
Classification: DDC 796.334--dc23

TABLE OF CONTENTS

A PERFECT NIGHT

It was early on a brisk mid-March evening in 2019 when Kendall Waston made his perfectly timed sprint. Waston was the first captain of FC Cincinnati—often referred to as FCC—in the team's brief history. He got himself behind a defender at the exact moment the ball arrived from about 35 yards (32 m) away. It was set in flight by a skillful free kick by teammate Leonardo Bertone.

"I just got on a run," Waston explained afterward, "and put my big head there."

Waston laughed. His leaping, lunging header during the 15th minute gave FC Cincinnati a lead in its first-ever home game. The goal set off a joyous explosion of cheers and celebration at Nippert Stadium.

Kendall Waston's header put FC Cincinnati on the scoreboard against Portland.

Waston, *center*, is mobbed by his teammates after his historic goal.

Cincinnati, at last, was home to Major League Soccer (MLS). The city's soccer fans had been looking forward to this game for a long time. It finally came on March 17, 2019, against the defending MLS Western Conference champion Portland Timbers.

The sellout crowd had been waving orange and blue flags and banners. They chanted and sang. Many began standing long before kickoff and remained on their feet all the way through the first 15 minutes of action.

MAKING HISTORY

Before Waston scored the team's first goal at home as part of MLS, it was hard to imagine the stadium getting any louder. But as soon as the ball skipped past a diving Portland goalkeeper, crossed the goal line, and settled into the left corner of the net, it did.

The FC Cincinnati players swarmed together for a group hug. Midfielder Roland Lamah turned to face the screaming fans. Lamah spread his arms out wide with his palms up, pumping them to the sky. It was his way of asking the crowd for even more noise.

Happy fans in the supporters' section, known as the Bailey, seemed to wave their rally towels even harder. A cloud of orange and blue powder covered them. It had been sprayed into the air around them as part of the celebration.

HAPPY DANCE

The night before the team's MLS home opener, the four-year-old son of FC Cincinnati's captain made up his own goal celebration. Little Keysaack Waston made his father promise he would use it. So when Kendall Waston scored the next day, he kept that promise. Waston lay down on his side and kicked his legs quickly, spinning himself around. In the joy of the moment, teammates copied Waston and performed the fun and oddball celebration too.

Waston's goal was perhaps the most memorable moment of FCC's first home game. But it would not be the only one during the 3–0 victory against the Timbers.

Adding to the thrill of the event, their first win as an MLS club was a shutout by goalkeeper Spencer Richey. Two of Richey's three saves came moments apart during the 32nd minute. The first was a diving stop on a hard, skipping shot by the Timbers' Bill Tuiloma. The second came from close range on a shot by Dairon Asprilla that had been set up by a corner kick.

But other than that one sequence, FC Cincinnati allowed Portland just one shot on goal. The Orange and Blue completely dominated the game, especially during the second half. They attempted 17 shots to just 10 for the Timbers.

Almost midway through that second half, FC Cincinnati scored two goals less than three minutes apart. Allan Cruz made it 2–0 with the highlight goal of the game. In the 61st minute, the team's star midfielder scored the first of what would be his team-best seven goals of the 2019 season. It was a backheel shot from the top of the six-yard box into a corner of the net. The ball had been deflected to Cruz off a shot from long range by Lamah.

Allan Cruz celebrates after giving FC Cincinnati a 2–0 lead.

Mathieu Deplagne then sealed the victory when he scored two minutes later off a cross-field pass from Darren Mattocks. It was the first MLS goal of Deplagne's career. The ball went into the net directly in front of the Bailey, where many of FCC's rowdiest supporters sit. The fans jumped up and down and hugged each other after each of the goals.

PARTY ATMOSPHERE

A few hours earlier, many of those fans had marched down West Charlton Street in a parade of supporters on their way to Nippert Stadium. The marchers took up the entire length of the four-lane street and stretched more than 100 yards (91 m) long. They sang, chanted, and screamed to the beat of drummers who walked along with them. Most wore the team's colors, and some sprayed orange and blue dust into the air.

Fans packed Nippert Stadium for the club's first MLS contest.

When the fans arrived at the stadium, some placed banners along the front rows of seats. Fans were treated to a special pregame ceremony that included a professional skydiving team dropping into the stadium to deliver the American flag before the National Anthem. It was all part of an incredible atmosphere created by the 32,250 fans in attendance, a record crowd for a league soccer game in Cincinnati.

"There was an extra buzz in the air tonight," Richey said. "I was getting the chills. It was as loud as I've ever heard it. It was pretty awesome."

Mattocks was in his eighth MLS season and had appeared in 166 league games before he was taken as FC Cincinnati's first pick of the expansion draft. Mattocks had played in almost every MLS stadium, in front of the rowdiest and most dedicated fans and supporters' sections all over the United States and Canada.

His first game in Cincinnati was enough to convince him the atmosphere at Nippert Stadium was one of the three best in the league. He said the crowd's support made it feel like the team had a 12th player on the field.

The players made sure they repaid the fans for their efforts. The Orange and Blue dominated one of the league's top teams in its first MLS home game.

"I'm very proud of our club, our city, and all the players," FCC head coach Alan Koch said. "I'm glad we could reward this city and our fans in a game that was very, very special to this community with a great performance."

Mathieu Deplagne, *left*, scored FCC's final goal of the day.

The rest of FC Cincinnati's first MLS season would not go as well as hoped. But those who were lucky enough to attend the team's first home game went home with a season's worth of good memories.

"It was a perfect, perfect night for the team," Deplagne said. "The crowd was perfect and the fans in the stadium pushed the group to be good and be perfect."

CHAPTER 2

FROM COMETS
TO KINGS

The dream of Major League Soccer in Cincinnati began three years before the city's first MLS game. That was when the city's team in the United Soccer League (USL) began play. The USL is a second-division league. FC Cincinnati played three seasons at that level.

Looking back at the USL version of FC Cincinnati, it had a lot in common with the MLS team of today. It had the same orange and blue color scheme and a similar logo. It also played home matches at Nippert Stadium on the campus of the University of Cincinnati.

The local fans quickly showed they were some of the best in the league. They set many USL attendance records. The team broke its own record for a USL regular-season crowd

FC Cincinnati midfielder Jimmy McLaughlin, left, heads the ball against Columbus Crew forward Adam Jahn during a US Open Cup match in 2017.

A record crowd at Nippert Field witnessed FCC's friendly with Crystal Palace in 2016.

several times. It also would break the record for biggest crowd at a league playoff game. Best of all, FC Cincinnati twice broke the USL season attendance record.

In 2016 FC Cincinnati hosted 35,061 fans for a friendly against Crystal Palace of the English Premier League. That was the largest crowd ever to watch a soccer game in Ohio at the time. This showed the US soccer community how much the people of Cincinnati liked the sport. It also impressed the people in charge of MLS. They saw that the city could support a team in soccer's first division.

But it wasn't just the fan support that made Cincinnati's USL team special. FCC won more games than it lost during all three seasons in the league. In 2018 the Orange and Blue's record of 23 wins, 3 losses, and 8 draws earned it the USL regular-season championship. The victory that clinched that honor was its ninth win in a row, a league record.

GIANT-KILLERS

FC Cincinnati's team in the USL also was known for its performance in the US Open Cup. The US Open Cup is a national tournament that allows clubs from all levels of play and leagues. MLS teams usually are far more successful in the tournament than teams from lower levels. But FCC beat two MLS teams during the 2017 tournament.

A US Open Cup semifinal match that year in Cincinnati drew 33,250 fans. And the Orange and Blue took a 2–0 lead against the MLS New York Red Bulls midway through the second half. A win would make FC Cincinnati only the third non-MLS team to reach the championship game since MLS began taking part in the tournament 21 years earlier. However, New York came from behind to pull out a 3–2 win.

MORE HISTORY

The history of professional soccer in Cincinnati goes back to a time long before FC Cincinnati began play. Twelve pro teams called Cincinnati home in the five decades before FCC's USL debut. The team that lasted the longest among those was the Cincinnati Kings. They played from 2005 to 2013. Also playing soccer in Cincinnati over those years were a variety of minor-league, indoor, and women's teams, including the Excite, the Saints, the Lady Saints, the Sirens and the Dutch Lions. The Dutch Lions kept playing even after FC Cincinnati was founded. They moved to Northern Kentucky University and joined a lower-level league.

The only other pro team to play in Nippert Stadium was the Comets. The Comets were members of the American Soccer League (ASL) from 1972 to 1975. In their first season, they won the league championship behind ASL most valuable player

The club's logo got a slight update before its MLS debut.

(MVP) Ringo Cantillo. The Comets were ASL runners-up in 1973, the only season they played at Nippert Stadium.

Indoor soccer soon became popular in the United States. Cincinnati had a Major Indoor Soccer League (MISL) team that

Cincinnati baseball legend Pete Rose tried to give indoor soccer a boost in 1978.

debuted when the league did in December 1978. Cincinnati played in the first MISL game ever. Baseball star Pete Rose was part-owner of the Cincinnati Kids. He was part of a ceremony before the first MISL game. Rose kicked out the first ball before the game between the Kids and New York Arrows.

The Kids lasted only one season. Pro soccer did not return to Cincinnati for 15 years. It would be another two decades after that before FC Cincinnati was born. But the success of the Orange and Blue came quickly. It was a reflection of the area's passionate soccer fans.

FOREVER THE
FIRSTS

Midfielder Allan Cruz quickly became a star for FC Cincinnati. Early on, he gained attention for his unique ability to score shortly after the start of a game.

Cruz scored in the Orange and Blue's first MLS game. He led the team in goals during that first MLS season with seven. And two of those seven goals came during the first minute of games. He became only the second player to score two first-minute goals in one season in league history. Four of Cruz's goals during the 2019 season came during the first 10 minutes of a match. Cruz led FCC that year in shots on goal with 21.

Cruz arrived in Cincinnati in 2019 after a transfer from a team in his native Costa Rica. He also made his debut for the

Allan Cruz found the back of the net early and often in 2019.

Fanendo Adi, *left*, battles with Penn FC's Walter Ramirez in a 2018 USL match.

Costa Rican national team when he was 22 years old. His first appearance for FC Cincinnati came six months later.

MLS rules limit the number of players on each team's roster that are not from the United States. Cruz was one of the first international players that the Orange and Blue signed.

The league also limits each team to three Designated Players. These are players who the team can sign outside of the league's salary cap. The first Designated Player that FC Cincinnati signed was Nigerian forward Fanendo Adi. He had scored 54 goals for the Portland Timbers over the previous five seasons. Adi joined FC Cincinnati in 2018 as the team was wrapping up its final USL season.

When the 2019 season began, Adi was part of the starting lineup for each of FC Cincinnati's first three MLS games. But he injured his ankle during the club's first MLS home game. Darren Mattocks took his place. Mattocks also has a spot in FC Cincy's history. He was the team's top pick in the MLS expansion draft. The speedy forward from Jamaica had played for DC United the year before.

EXPANSION PICKS

The expansion draft is one way that new teams joining a league can fill their rosters. Each of the existing teams can protect a certain number of players in their organization. The expansion teams then select players who were left unprotected. FC Cincinnati also took midfielder Roland Lamah of FC Dallas in the expansion draft. Lamah, a native of Ivory Coast, was one of the Orange and Blue's top midfielders during their first MLS season.

The team's best midfielder that historic first year was Emmanuel Ledesma. He led the team with five assists and 49 shots. Ledesma was second on the team in goals with six. He holds a special place in FC Cincinnati history. He was the best player in the USL during the Orange and Blue's final season in that league. It was 2018, the year before FCC joined MLS. Ledesma had 16 goals and set a USL record with 16 assists. He was named league Player of the Month twice and earned the USL MVP award that season.

Emmanuel Ledesma continued his excellent play when FCC made the jump from the USL to MLS.

OTHER FIRSTS

That wasn't the only award FC Cincinnati won during its final season before joining MLS. Alan Koch was named the USL Coach of the Year. Koch was the MLS team's first coach, too.

Kendall Waston was FCC's first captain. Przemyslaw Tytoń was the goalkeeper for its first game. Waston, Tytoń, and the others on the Orange and Blue's first MLS team were there because of Jeff Berding. Berding had been the club's president and general manager.

Early in the team's first MLS season, Berding hired Gerard Nijkamp to take over as general manager. Nijkamp built the club for its second MLS season. Two of the best players he acquired before that season were high-scoring forwards Yuya Kubo and Jurgen Locadia. Kubo is from Japan and Locadia from the Netherlands. Each was a Designated Player for FC Cincinnati during the 2020 season. Locadia scored a goal during his first game for the club. Kubo scored in his second game and went on to lead the team in goals.

Mathieu Deplagne and Spencer Richey played every minute of both of those games. That was not surprising because both were important players in FCC's first MLS campaign.

Jurgen Locadia, *right*, battles for position in a 2020 match against Atlanta United.

Spencer Richey was FC Cincinnati's top goalkeeper in the club's first MLS season.

Deplagne was one of the most durable members of the club. He started the first 27 matches, and he played every minute of the first 17 games in the Orange and Blue's first MLS season. The defender from France led the club in starts, games, and minutes played.

Richey was a holdover from the USL days. The Seattle native started 19 of 34 matches and was in the net for five of the team's six victories in 2019. However, he lost the starting job to Tytoń in 2020 and wasn't re-signed. Tytoń, from Poland, had five shutouts in 12 starts that year.

Cruz will be forever known as the MVP of FCC's first MLS entry. Cruz signed a multi-year contract extension after the 2019 season. Fans of the Orange and Blue are excited to watch him create many more memories in years to come.

JOE GYAU

Joe Gyau showed enough talent as a teenager that he signed with a team in Germany's Bundesliga, one of the top leagues in Europe. But Gyau wasn't given much playing time and ended up bouncing around Germany's lower-level leagues. After nine years in Germany, FC Cincinnati signed the midfielder before the club's inaugural season. Gyau earned a regular place in the lineup by 2020, playing 21 matches and scoring one goal.

CHAPTER 4

'WELCOME, FC CINCINNATI!'

Supporters chanted and marched and cheered. Approximately 1,000 of them packed into a large restaurant hall on a Tuesday afternoon. But it was not for a match. It was just for an announcement. On May 29, 2018, MLS commissioner Don Garber told the gathered soccer fans that it would be a day they would never forget.

"This is the moment that you've all been waiting for, and we have been anticipating for so long," Garber said joyfully. "Ladies and gentlemen, it is my great pleasure to announce that Cincinnati, Ohio, is officially granted the newest expansion club in Major League Soccer. Welcome, FC Cincinnati!"

FC Cincinnati supporters celebrated when the team was officially welcomed to MLS.

THE PRI
UTD

Shovels are lined up at the ground-breaking ceremony for FC Cincinnati's new West End Stadium on December 18, 2018.

The crowd erupted in a loud cheer. Soccer fans in Cincinnati had wanted this for a long time. Their support of the USL team proved that the city of Cincinnati deserved an MLS club. Now they finally would be able to say their club was part of the top professional soccer league in North America.

Seven months after Cincinnati was officially awarded a team, a ground-breaking ceremony was held for a place for it to play. Construction of the West End Stadium was at last underway. It would host FC Cincinnati games for years to come. It was built at a cost of $250 million. The Orange and Blue's new home was designed to hold 26,000 fans.

MLS DEBUT

Nippert Stadium would remain FC Cincinnati's home for the club's first two seasons in MLS. The club's first game, however, would be played more than 2,000 miles away. It was in Seattle on March 2, 2019. A crowd of 39,011 was at CenturyLink Field that day. The Seattle Sounders were a strong team. They would go on to win the MLS Cup that year.

Their ability showed as Seattle beat FC Cincinnati 4–1. The defeat did not take away from what was a special day for everyone who was a part of the franchise, however. Owner Carl Lindner III and president Jeff Berding had worked hard to get FC Cincinnati to that point. Both had been with the organization since it was founded as a USL team four years earlier.

The ending wasn't what they were hoping for, but at least the Orange and Blue took a lead in their first game. Swiss midfielder Leonardo Bertone scored one of the fastest goals scored for any MLS expansion team in history. Bertone struck

in the 13th minute. It was a goal worthy of highlight reels. Bertone's shot was a full volley from more than 20 yards (18 m) away from the goal.

STAYING POWER

FC Cincinnati's first point in the MLS standings came eight days later during its second MLS match. The Orange and Blue played defending MLS Cup champion Atlanta United to a 1–1 draw. The game was on the road in the massive Mercedes-Benz

Supporters in the Bailey raised their scarves and sang at FCC's first MLS home match.

Stadium. Midfielder Roland Lamah scored in the 86th minute to earn a point for FCC.

Two weeks later, Cincinnati soccer fans were excited. Their team had already won its home opener. Then, it improved to 2–1–1 after a 2–0 road victory against the New England Revolution. Kekuta Manneh and Kenny Saief each tallied a goal and an assist for the Orange and Blue. Meanwhile, goalkeeper

Spencer Richey posted a second straight shutout in that victory.

Unfortunately, FC Cincinnati would win only one of its next 14 matches. But the Orange and Blue did have success against one of the better teams in the league that year. They beat the Montreal Impact twice, including a May 11 home victory when Montreal was in first place in the Eastern Conference. It was Yoann Damet's first game as FC Cincinnati's interim coach. Alan Koch had been relieved of his duties during the team's long cold spell.

Allan Cruz scored during the seventh minute against Montreal. No goal all season showed more teamwork from Orange and Blue. Cruz's one-touch shot flipped up into the crossbar on the left side of the net. It was assisted by Darren Mattocks. Mattocks' pass was the 16th in a row by FC Cincinnati players. They had possession for more than a minute leading up to the goal. Fatai Alashe's goal in the 62nd minute helped clinch a 2–1 victory.

Defender Greg Garza plays the ball during FC Cincinnati's victory over the Montreal Impact in May 2019.

The last win of FC Cincinnati's first MLS season was against Montreal, too. Cruz scored a first-minute goal, pouncing on a deflected shot and knocking it past Montreal goalkeeper Evan Bush. That was it for the scoring that day as FCC held on for a

Kekuta Manneh, *right*, blasts home the winning goal against Louisville FC in the club's 2019 US Open Cup match.

1–0 victory. Backup keeper Przemyslaw Tytoń made one save for one of his three clean sheets of the season.

FC Cincinnati won just two MLS games in the four months between the two victories against Montreal. The wins came together a week apart in July. The first was at home on July 6 against the Houston Dynamo. Manneh, Rashawn Dally, and

Victor Ulloa scored goals in the 3–2 win. Richey finished the game with a black, bloody eye after being cleated in the face.

Seven days later, the Orange and Blue made it two in a row. Cruz again scored during the first minute. Fanendo Adi added a goal during the final minutes. Adi's first goal all MLS season for FC Cincinnati was timely. It came during the 83rd minute to break a tie and give FC Cincinnati a 2–1 win at the Chicago Fire.

TOURNAMENT SUCCESS

One noteworthy victory during FC Cincinnati's first year as an MLS club did not come in MLS play. It came June 12 against Louisville City FC during the US Open Cup tournament. The teams had formed a rivalry during three seasons in the USL. This game allowed for a renewal of what had come to be known as the Dirty River Derby.

Fans often made the 90-minute drive between Louisville and Cincinnati for games. Some Louisville supporters traveled to Nippert Stadium for this match. The Orange and Blue won 2–1 when Manneh scored in extra time. Adi had a goal in the first half.

The Orange and Blue didn't get a chance to compete in the 2020 US Open Cup. The tournament was canceled due to the

COVID-19 pandemic. The MLS season took a four-month pause as well. It resumed with a tournament of a different type in Orlando called MLS Is Back.

Cincinnati had some motivation for its first game. It was a meeting with rival Columbus. But the northerners came away with an easy 4–0 victory. The 2020 season was already looking like a disaster.

But in its next game, Cincinnati scored a 1–0 upset over reigning US Open Cup champs Atlanta United. Then FCC knocked off the New York Red Bulls 2–0 to advance out of the group stage. In the knockout round, a late tying goal from Jurgen Locadia forced a penalty shootout against the Portland Timbers. But the Orange and Blue lost the shootout 4–2.

That was the highlight of a difficult 2020 season. Cincinnati won just two more games and finished at the bottom of MLS. And because of the pandemic, it couldn't

play in front of its loyal fans. The club and its fans looked forward to opening West End Stadium and making memories for seasons to come.

TIMELINE

2015	2016	2016	2016	2017
On August 12, FC Cincinnati is announced as a new entry in the USL.	FC Cincinnati plays its first game as a franchise, a 2–2 draw with KR Reykjavík on February 20, as part of a preseason tournament in Florida.	In its second home game, FC Cincinnati sets a single-game USL attendance record of 20,497 for a match against Louisville FC on April 16.	FC Cincinnati falls 2–0 in a friendly against English club Crystal Palace on July 16 before 35,061 fans, the largest crowd to see a soccer match in the state of Ohio.	FCC hosts the New York Red Bulls of MLS in a US Open Cup semifinal on August 15. Although it had beaten two other MLS clubs during the tournament, FCC loses 3–2.

2018	2018	2019	2019	2020
Cincinnati is awarded an MLS expansion franchise on May 29.	FC Cincinnati clinches the USL regular-season title on September 26 in its last season in the league.	FC Cincinnati loses its first MLS match 4–1 at Seattle on March 2.	On March 17 FCC defeats the Portland Timbers 3–0 in their first home MLS match.	FC Cincinnati advances out of the group stage at the MLS Is Back tournament in Orlando.

TEAM FACTS

FIRST SEASON

2019

STADIUMS

Nippert Stadium (2019–20)
West End Stadium (2021–)

KEY PLAYERS

Allan Cruz (2019–)
Yuya Kubo (2020–)
Jurgen Locadia (2020–)
Spencer Richey (2019–20)
Kendall Waston (2019–20)

KEY COACHES

Yoann Damet (2019–20)
Alan Koch (2019)
Jaap Stam (2020–)

NON-MLS SEASONS

3 (2016–18 in USL)

USL MOST VALUABLE PLAYERS

Emmanuel Ledesma (2018)
Sean Okoli (2016)

GLOSSARY

backheel
A kick played by the heel, typically traveling in the opposite direction from where the player is facing.

clean sheet
A shutout, or a match in which the opposing team does not score.

commissioner
The person who is in charge of a sports league, making major decisions about the organization and resolving disputes among its teams.

Designated Player
An MLS player whose salary does not count against the league's salary cap.

draw
A game that ends in a tie.

free kick
An unguarded kick awarded to a team after an opponent's foul.

friendly
A match that is not part of league play or a tournament; an exhibition match.

general manager
An executive who runs a team and is responsible for finding and signing players.

salary cap
A limit on the amount of money that teams can pay players.

MORE INFORMATION

BOOKS

Avise, Jonathan. *Great Soccer Debates*. Minneapolis, MN: Abdo Publishing, 2019.

Carothers, Thomas. *Columbus Crew SC*. Minneapolis, MN: Abdo Publishing, 2022.

Marthaler, Jon. *US Men's Professional Soccer*. Minneapolis, MN: Abdo Publishing, 2019.

ONLINE RESOURCES

To learn more about FC Cincinnati, please visit **abdobooklinks.com** or scan this QR code. These links are routinely monitored and updated to provide the most current information available.

INDEX

ABOUT THE AUTHOR

A 20-year veteran of sports journalism, Chris Adamski joined the *Pittsburgh Tribune-Review* in 2012. His primary beat has been coverage of the Steelers since 2014. He also has been responsible for covering the Penguins and Penn State football. Adamski has lived in Pittsburgh since graduating from Penn State in 2002 after earning two bachelor's degrees, including one in journalism. He is married with four children.